LOCO-HAULED

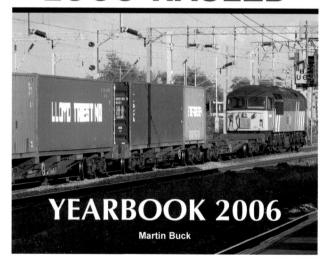

YEARBOOK 2006

Martin Buck

FREIGHTMASTER

PUBLISHING

CONTENTS

Published by :

Freightmaster Publishing
158 Overbrook
SWINDON
SN3 6AY

01793 - 644957

www.freightmasterpublishing.co.uk

First published : January 2007

ISBN : 0 - 9537540 - 7 - 3

Printed By :

Stephens & George
Goat Mill Road
Dowlais
MERTHYR TYDFIL
CF48 3TD

Cover Design : Martin Buck

PREFACE

Loco-Hauled Yearbook - 2006 is the sequel to 'Railfreight Yearbook - 2005' published last Spring, with the aim of providing a pictorial record of the railfreight and loco-hauled passenger highlights of 2006, including a touch of mainline steam as well!

There have been many highlights and it just goes to show how varied and interesting the railway scene is in the UK, which I hope will be borne out in the forthcoming pages. There are too many events to record here, but a few highlights are worthy of mention:-

- Launch of the Blue Pullman

- Freightliner Aggregate/Scrap Metal gains

- Isambard Kingdom Brunel Bi-centennial

- GBRf 'Metronet' Class 66/7s

- Fastline's Class 56 intermodals

- Class 50s on the mainline

- NMT Substitute HST

- FM Rail's move into freight

- EWS in France

- Launch of Stobart Rail

- DRS and Heritage Class 47's

I would like to thank all the people who hav kindly contributed material for consideration; have been simply inundated with image resulting in a laborious (but rewarding) task c whittling them down to this final selection.

This pictorial record is based entirely on th images submitted and I offer an apology if ar 'highlights' have been overlooked. Wherev possible, I have attempted to include at lea one image from each contributor and trust th such fine imagery will place the contributors the 'shop window' for all to see.

Finally, compilation has been a pleasure a I hope *Loco-Hauled Yearbook - 2006* v result in a similar title for 2007!

Martin Bu

JANUARY

Banbury Road Stone Terminal

Situated three miles north of Oxford on the Bicester line, the long-disused Banbury Road stone terminal reopens, taking over some of the traffic formerly handled at Appleford tip. The loaded train will run in the same path, although the empties return later.

Both trains run via Swindon and a rake of MendipRail JNA bogie box wagons will be used for the service, running as:

6A13, 06:55 (SX) Westbury Yard - Oxford Banbury Road
6C53, 12:59 (SX) Oxford Banbury Road - Whatley

(Right) : **Class 66/0 No. 66071 negotiates Didcot North Junction on 20 June with a rake of JNAs loaded with stone forming 6A13, Westbury - Banbury Road.**

(Below) : **On the following day, Class 60 No. 60082 is unusually rostered to work the train, seen at the terminal itself, with the JNA's in the process of being unloaded.**

The actual diagram is 'booked' for an EWS Class 59/2 locomotive.

(Both Ian Ball)

'Blue Pullman'

One recalls the 1960's DEMU which used to work passenger services between Paddington and Cardiff, also between London St. Pancras and Manchester Central in the famed, striking, colours of Nanking blue and white. Well, the 'Blue Pullman' is back - a FM Rail creation - formed of Mk. II air-conditioned coaching stock and two Class 47/7 locomotives, Nos. 47709 *Dionysos* and 47712 *Artemis* operating in top 'n' tail mode.

Twelve coaches are being turned out in the 'Blue Pullman' colours, although the train set will normally comprise eight vehicles. This magnificent train will work throughout the network and, as we shall see, capture the imagination of railway photographers across the land.

(Above) : **On the day of the official launch, 5 January, rather overcast conditions are met by the cameraman as he records Class 47/7 No. 47712 *Artemis* top 'n' tailing No. 47709 *Dyonisos* as The Blue Pullman passes Levenshulme heading from Derby to Manchester Piccadilly.** *(Alan Sherratt)*

Port Talbot Scrap

A new traffic flow this month sees the movement of scrap metal to the Corus steelworks at Port Talbot. Up to five trains can run each week, from three different sources:

    6Z71, 06:52 (ThSO) Margam - Washwood Heath
    6G73, 04:44 (MFO)   Washwood Heath - Handsworth
    6G74, 15:53 (MFO)   Handsworth - Margam

    6Z71, 06:52 (TO)   Margam - Washwood Heath
    6Z72, 12:10 (TThO) Healey Mills - Margam   (wagons are loaded at Laisterdyke)

    6H55, 06:52 (WFO) Margam - Swindon
    6H56, 17:19 (WO)   Swindon - Margam

You will notice that the workings don't appear to balance and this is because the Friday morning empties to Swindon then form a loaded train to Liverpool and are tripped from there to Healey Mills in the early hours of Monday morning, ready to be loaded at Laisterdyke.

Buffer-Fitted HTAs

Class 60s are now seeing regular use with buffer-fitted HTA sets that, until fitted with buffers, could only be hauled by 66s. The relevant HTA hoppers have had 20,000 added to their original number, becoming:

330191   330215   330331
330332   330381   330745

(Right) : **Amidst a fine array of semaphore signals at Barnetby, Class 60 No. 60063 *James Murray* heads 4C72 Scunthorpe - Immingham 'Buffer-fitted' HTA empties.** *(Ian Ball)*

FGW 'Duff' Sleepers

First Great Western get off to a bad start in 2006, suffering major non-availability of their Class 57/6 fleet, and have to hire-in substitute traction in the shape of Cotswold Rail's No. 47813 *John Peel*, which is thrust into action on 24 January when it leaves Penzance atop 1A40, 22:00 Penzance - Paddington overnight sleeper; the locomotive running light engine from Gloucester to work the train! Upon arrival at Paddington, the ECS (5A40) is hauled to Old Oak Common by another Class 47, No. 47840 *North Star* - when was the last time Paddington played host to two Class 47s?

On 24 January, No. 47840 is summoned to Newbury to rescue No. 57605 *Totnes Castle* (traction motor failure) while working (HST substitute) 1A86, 09:04 Penzance - Paddington.

The problems culminate during 1 February and the early hours of the following morning when No. 57603 *Tintagel Castle* suffers loss of power at Penzance on 1A40 sleeper and two FGW power cars Nos. 43165 and 43187 (in back-to-back formation) are allocated to work the train. At Plymouth, the power cars are replaced by Cotswold Rail No. 47828, summoned from Gloucester, which works the train forward to Bristol Temple Meads, where No. 57604 *Pendennis Castle* takes over.

(Above) : **A first for the new year; a Class 47 unexpectedly arrives at London Paddington in the early hours of the morning on 25 January when Cotswold Rail's Class 47/8 No. 47818 *John Peel* works in with 1A40, 22:00 Penzance - Paddington sleeper, substituting for the booked class 57/6 locomotive.** *(Marc Ely)*

6V91

(Above) : One of a handful of 'Scrappers' to run this year, sees celebrity Class 47/8 No. 47840 *North Star* pass Cholsey on 17 January with 6V91, Shoeburyness - Newport Docks and VEP's 3486/3530/3490 in tow, destined for MoD Caerwent following asbestos and component removal at Shoeburyness.   *(Marc Ely)*

ED 'On Hire'

(Below) : GBRf hire The Class 73 Locomotive Preservation Company's Class 73 No. 73136 (E6043) *Perseverance*. E6043 for infrastructure duties in Sussex and the immaculate ED is seen pausing at Redhill on 21 January after running round 6G13, 21:20 Hoo Junction - Gatwick Airport, paired with recent GBRf purchase No. 73208, still in Gatwick Express livery.   *(Marc Ely)*

S. & C. Diversions

(Above) : The WCML closes over the weekend of 21-22 January and both freight and passenger services are diverted via the 'Settle & Carlisle'. Thunderbird' Class 57/3 No. 57303 *Alan Tracy* drags Pendolino No. 390002 *Virgin Angel* on 21 January on the approach to Settle Junction with VWC's diverted 1M16, 11:40 Glasgow - Euston (due 2011 after a further diversion via the West Midlands - Note, there is only enough room for one photographer in the tree on the left of the picture!   *(Peter Kellett)*

(Below) : Same day, same location and EWS Class 92 No. 92029 *Dante* makes what is thought to be the first appearance by a class member on the S & C, dead in the consist of EWS's late running 6M76, 21:34 Mossend - Warrington 'Enterprise', hauled by Class 66/0 No. 66073.   *(Andrew Naylor)*

London Excursions .....

(Above) : HSBC Rail Class 86/2 No. 86212 is moved on 31 January from Oxley (Wolverhampton) to East Ham depot for 'pre-heating' duties by Class 31/1 No. 31190 *Gryphon,* running as 0Z59, 10:00 Oxley - East Ham EMD, seen passing Camden Road. *(Iain Scotchman)*

(Below) : The following day, the weather takes a turn for the worse as Class 67 No. 67021 arrives at London Charing Cross station with 1Z14, 09.51 ex-Hither Green Serco test train; No. 67024 is on the rear (not visible); the London Eye and Millennium Bridge being the notable landmarks in view. *(Iain Scotchman)*

'Blue Pullman' Southern Style

(Above) : The new Blue Pullman will become a familiar sight around the regions as demand for its use increases throughout 2006. We begin with a sojourn onto Southern metals and the celebrity train locomotives Nos. 47712 *Artemis* & 47709 *Dyonisos* Top & tail 1Z83, 12:30 Folkestone Harbour - Victoria (via Dungeness) passing Dollands Moor on 4 February.   *(Iain Scotchman)*

(Below) : On their third visit on Southern metals, Nos. 47709 and 47712 power 1Z40, 09:20 Stevenage - Salisbury 'Blue Pullman' up the bank, away from Virginia Water on Valentines Day.   *(Chris Nevard)*

To The Rescue

(Above) : Following the derailment of Class 66/0 No. 66017 at Melton Mowbray, the Old Oak Common breakdown train is summoned! At 14:59 hrs. on 9 February, Class 37/4 No. 37411 *Caerphilly Castle* passes Kilby Bridge Junction, near Leicester, forming 1Z99, the 11:45 Old Oak Common - Melton Mowbray; perhaps, the 'working of the year' on the Midland Mainline'! *(Andy Small)*

Sweet Dreams

(Below) : Due to engineering work between Tulloch and Bridge of Orchy, the WHL sleeper is diverted away from Fort William and Class 37/4 No. 37406 *The Saltire Society* stands proud at Oban with 1B01, 19:43 (Sun) Oban - Edinburgh on 19 February. McCaig's Folly is beautifully lit in the background. *(Adrian Kenny)*

Barry 'ED'

(Above) : GB Railfreight Class 66/7 No. 66714 *Cromer Lifeboat* makes history on 20 February as the first GBRf locomotive to reach Barry. It is seen in the siding adjacent to Barry station having arrived with 5Z77, 10:32 Stewarts Lane - Barry ECS, formed of ex-Gatwick Express Mk. II stock.   *(Mark Thomas)*

(Below) : Mainline certified Class 73/1 No. 73136 *Perseverance*, which was on the rear of 5Z77, shunts the stock at the former EWS sheds at Barry, prior to working the stock on to Barry Island Railway metals. The stock comprises sets 8206/8311/9110 (vehicles 68509, 72505, 72620/1/9 and 72710) and having been withdrawn from service in 2005, Porterbrook have now disposed of the last remaining former Gatwick Express stock. The Barry Island Railway have plans to use the vehicles in push-pull mode with preserved ED No. 73133 on a new line extension.   *(Mark Thomas)*

Welsh Whistler

(Above) : Fond memories are rekindled as CFPS Class 40 No. 40145 passes through Newport station on 25 February working the 'Welsh Whistler', 1Z47, 06:01 Crewe - Cardiff charter. In fact, it is some 25 years since the author last recorded a run behind this locomotive - 12 June, 1982 - from Chester to Llandudno Junction on 1D35, 09:45 Manchester Victoria - Bangor. ***(Mark Thomas)***

6V91 (again!)

(Below) : Another 'Scrapper', but an unusual choice of traction, to say the least! GBRf find themselves short of a 66/7 to work 6V91, Shoeburyness - Newport Docks on 28 February and hire FGW Class 57/6 No. 57604 *Pendennis Castle,* seen at Pilning with CIG's 1866/1805 and various vehicles from VEPs 3485/3489/3568. ***(Adrian Kenny)***

EPS 'Drags'

(Above) : EPS driver training 'Drags' take place in March, providing the welcome sight of the Eurostar Class 37/6 pool hauling 18-coach Class 373 units. Although booked for a pair of 'Tractors', occasionally a lone example will deputise as on 15 March when No. 37601 approaches Tonbridge leading an unidentified Eurostar set on 5X11, 13:31 Dollands Moor - North Pole.   *(Marc Ely)*

Sweet Caroline

(Below) : Reminiscent of when Class 33 locomotives were regular performers on the Barnstaple branch, 'Push-Pull' No. 33103 *Swordfish* propels the Network Rail inspection saloon No. 975025 *Caroline* past Abbot's Marsh, near Portsmouth Arms, on 16 March, running as 2Z33, 09:35 Exeter St. David's - Barnstaple. The saloon is a former 'Hastings Line' DEMU buffet car.   *(Dave Mitchell)*

The Last Pipes

(Above) : This month sees the cessation of the 'Stanton Pipes'. On 1 March, Class 60 No. 60003 *Freight Transport Association* passes Toton Junction heading for Long Eaton and then Derby en-route to Teesside with 6E77, Stanton Gate - Tees Yard loaded pipes.   *(Don Gatehouse)*

Wirral Serco

(Below) : The mainline between Shotton (High Level) and Bidston does not see any loco-hauled activity, so 14 March proves to be a real bonus. Class 67 No. 67028 Top 'n' tails No. 67011 (out of view) as it passes Heswall, 6 miles into its journey, heading a Bidston - Wrexham Serco Test Train.   *(Fred Kerr)*

Rare Track

(Above) : Any locomotive on the curve from Hatton West Junction to Hatton North Junction is exceptionally unusual as the line is normally only used by a daily DMU ECS to Stratford-upon-Avon. So, when Class 60 No. 60096 turned up on 6P04, Bearley Junction - Bescot engineers train, it made 19 March something of a red-letter day. Sadly, a suicide took place under this train later in the afternoon at Olton.   *(Peter Tandy)*

(Below) : Meanwhile, on the same day, Class 66/0 No. 66098 passes through Claverdon station, on the Stratford-upon-Avon branch with a 6P06 ballast from Bescot to Bearley; another extremely rare section for locomotive hauled activity!   *(Peter Tandy)*

Winwick Wonders

(Above) : On 22 March, Freightliner's Class 47/8 No. 47830 passes Winwick Junction, north of Warrington, in the process of moving a crippled HHA coal hopper from Mossend to Crewe Basford Hall.   *(Fred Kerr)*

(Below) : Later that day, the variety continues when 6F30, Castleton - Arpley departmental passes the same location with no less than three Class 67s on the front - Nos. 67024, 67022 and 67015.   *(Fred Kerr)*

Southport 'Freds'

(Above) : This is a rare sight, a close-up view of two Freightliner Class 66/5 locomotives stabled at Southport, Nos. 66547 and No. 66522, on 26 March whilst in the process of removing redundant track from Birkdale PW site.
(Fred Kerr)

6A30

(Above) : 6A30, Mossend - Aberdeen 'Enterprise was always a good provider of 'classic' traction and even into 2006 it still provides the occasional highlight. The service has been boosted by the inclusion of calcium traffic, fortunately in the load on 23 March when Class 37/4 No. 37417 *Richard Trevithick* leads sister locomotive No. 37427, as the staple diet of pipes on BDA's is missing. The pair pass Larbert Junction with The Falkirk Wheel visible in the background. *(Peter Kellett)*

'87' Lament

(Below) : Cotswold Rail are summoned on 30 March to provide traction for 0Z03, Bicester COD - Long Marston move of withdrawn Class 87s Nos. 87009/020/034. Class 47s Nos. 47714 + 47813 *John Peel* are seen passing Evesham signalbox with the 87s in tow, running via Oxford, Swindon, Kemble and Worcester, where the locos run-round before heading south on the Cotswold line. *(Peter Tandy)*

APRIL

Blueberry Fool

(Below) : On 1 April, Hertfordshire Railtours run the "Blueberry Fool" from London Cannon Street to Hastings, Brighton and Littlehampton via Tonbridge and returning to London Bridge via the mid-Sussex line and Epsom. Two EDs, Nos. 73136 *Perseverance* and 73107 *Spitfire* provide the traction with the former leading, approaching High Brooms station between Tonbridge and Tunbridge Wells.   *(Alan Hazelden)*

(Bottom) : An elevated view of the same train, 1Z73, 09:35 Cannon Street - Littlehampton, curving off London Road viaduct to join the Brighton Mainline with No. 73136 leading the ensemble.   *(Marc Ely)*

19

APRIL

Bardon Aggregates

Effective from the first day of the month, Freightliner *Heavy Haul* have beaten off competition from EWS to secure a five year contract to move aggregates from the quarries at Bardon Hill and Croft, from Wool and also Jersey Marine and Neath in South Wales.

The flows affected are:

- Bardon Hill to Thorney Mill
- Bardon Hill to Brentford
- Bardon Hill to Washwood Heath

- Bardon Hill to Harlow Mill
- Bardon Hill to Angerstein

- Croft to Bow

- Croft to Neasden

- Wool to Neasden

- Jersey Marine to Thorney Mill

-Jersey Marine to Angerstein

Consequently, the Bardon and Croft trains retain the same headcodes, but the Wool and Jersey Marine traffic is recast. One of the features of these new Freightliner flows is the variety of wagons used to convey aggregate between the quarry/loading point and receiving terminals; a selection of four wagon types are illustrated here.

(Left) : This is Bow Goods, adjacent to the Great Eastern Mainline, where Class 66/6 No. 66609 waits to leave on 12 April with 6M47 empty JRAs to Croft. These blue (ex-Camas) JRAs, built in 1990, are internationally registered in the (RIV) 33. 70. 6905. 050 to 073 range. *(Iain Scotchman)*

(Bottom Left) : The Wool sand train uses 2-Axle PGA wagons in the VTG 14203 - 14461 number range. Class 66/5 No. 66518 passes Trumps Mill Lane, Virginia Water, on 24 August with 6O49, Neasden - Wool sand empties. *(Chris Nevard)*

(Top Right) : A truly delightful scene, amidst a sea of oilseed rape, the unmistakable 'Shanks-liveried' Class 66/5 locomotive No. 66522 passes Harrowden Junction, just north of Wellingborough, on 11 May with 6M17, Croft - Neasden loaded hoppers. These JGA hoppers are ex-RH Roadstone and numbered within the FLHL17302 to 17324 range. *(John Rudd)*

(Bottom Right) : Class 66/5 No. 66514 passes the site of Ashbury level crossing near Shrivenham with a rake of empty PGA wagons (VTG 14346 to 14385 number range) on 6B11, Thorney Mill - Cardiff Pengam *(Martin Buck)*

Isambard Kingdom Brunel - 200

April 9th. 2006, marks the 200th. anniversary of the birth of arguably the greatest railway engineer - Isambard Kingdom Brunel - who according to a TV poll in 2002 is the second greatest Briton ever. To commemorate the event, there will be a series of special steam-hauled trains in celebration. As a mark of appreciation, here is a brief resume of his life and achievements:

1806 : Born 9 April at Portsea, near Portsmouth, the only son of a French civil engineer.

1823 : Worked with his father on the design and build of the Thames Tunnel, London.

1829 : Designed the River Avon suspension bridge.

1831 : Appointed chief engineer at Bristol Docks and went on to design the Docks at Cardiff, Milford Haven and Plymouth.

1833 : Appointed chief engineer of the Great Western Railway - highlights being:
- The 'Broad Gauge' main line between London and Bristol
- Hanwell Viaduct, Maidenhead Bridge, Box Tunnel and Bristol Temple Meads station.

1838 : Maiden voyage to New York of his Steam Boat the 'Great Western' - at the time the longest steamship in existence at 236 feet long.

1845 : Maiden voyage of 'Great Britain' from Liverpool to New York, the first propeller driven ship.

1852 : Employed by the Eastern Steam Navigation Company to build the paddle-wheel 'Great Eastern' and, during her sea trials in 1859, Brunel suffered a seizure.

1859 : Opening of the Royal Albert railway bridge across the River Tamar on 2 May.

1859 : Brunel dies on 15 September and is buried in Kensal Green cemetery.

Above) : On 8 April, King class 4-6-0 No. 6024 'King Edward I' passes Filton with 1Z53, 09:34 Bristol Temple Meads - Shrewsbury at the start of the year long Brunel 200 celebrations. *(Matt Turner)*

Top Left) : On the Great Western Mainline, 'King Edward I' passes Shrivenham on 3 July with another celebratory special, 1Z24, 10:50 Paddington - Bristol Temple Meads. *(Martin Buck}*

Bottom Left) : Here, the "King" attacks the climb to Savernake on 25 June with 13 coaches of "The Bristolian" at Crofton, alongside the Kennet & Avon Canal. The train starts its journey diesel-hauled from Ashford to Willesden SW Sidings where the "King" takes over. *(Geoff Plumb)*

Scrap Metal

Hot on the heals of the Bardon traffic gain, Freightliner *Heavy Haul* have wln the scrap metal flow from Beeston to Cardiff:

6Z97, 12:45 (TThSO) Beeston - Cardiff Tidal	6Z98, 06:30 (MO) Cardiff Tidal - Beeston
	6Z98, 19:20 (WFO) Cardiff Tidal - Beeston

However, the trains from Plymouth, Saltley, Kingsbury, Handsworth and Tyne Dock to Cardiff are still operated by EWS and the long-suspended scrap workings to Sheerness restart on Monday, 3 April:

Willesden - Sheerness (three trains a week)   Snailwell - Sheerness (Weekly)

(Right) : The new flow is routed via the Welsh Marches line, but on Saturday, 15 July, Class 66/5 No. 66531 passes the cameraman at Ashchurch hauling 6Z97, 11:50 Beeston - Cardiff Tidal loaded scrap.   *(Peter Tandy)*

(Top Right) : This view shows Class 66/6 No. 66608 on 6Z97 passing the delightful Stokesay Castle at Craven Arms on 29 April en-route to Cardiff Tidal.   *(Nick Slocombe)*

(Bottom Right) : With the London Eye in the background, Class 66/0 No. 66187 passes through Nunhead on 3 April with the first run of the reinstated 6O65, Willesden - Sheerness.   *(Nick Slocombe)*

(Below) : A housing estate now sits on the site of the former freightliner terminal at Pengam, Cardiff, where Class 66/5 No. 66530 passes with 6Z97, 11:50 Beeston - Cardiff Tidal loaded scrap on Saturday, 3 June. The consist is a rake of 20 VTG JNA bogie box wagons.   *(Adrian Kenny)*

'Metronet' Class 66s

On 8 April, five Class 66/7s which will work on the London Underground Metronet infrastructure renewal scheme arrive at Newport Docks from Canada on the MV Jumbo Challenger. The five are part of an £80 million, ten-year deal between Metronet (the company responsible for London Underground sub-surface lines) and GBRf, who operate the locomotives.

The five Class 66/7 locos. are numbered 66718 to 66722 and each carries the Metronet livery with the words 'Renewing the Tube' on the side panels. The fleet will be based at Wellingborough on the Midland Mainline and will work on the Metropolitan, District and Piccadilly Lines that can be accessed from Network Rail points at Amersham, Harrow-on-the-Hill, Gunnersby, East Putney and Wimbledon.

As part of this work, GBRf will be taking delivery of a total of 147 new wagons/vehicles, including:

- 22 FEA Bogie Flat Wagons

- 10 HQA Autoballasters

- 90 JNA "Falcon' Low-Sided Bogie Box Wagons

- 25 MRA Side-Tipping Bogie Wagons

(Top) : On a dreadfully dull day, as is so often the case when seeking to photograph the arrival of new locomotives, the convoy of 'Metronet' Class 66/7s passes through Swindon on 11 April en-route to their new home, running as 0M06, 12:25 Newport Docks - Willesden. *(Martin Buck*

(Above) : As well as their intended use on London Underground engineering work, the new locos. find gainful employment around the country on a variety of duties, as illustrated here. No. 66722 arrives at Selby Potters Yard on 31 May with 4E78, Felixstowe - Selby intermodal. *(Ian Ball*

(Top Right) : Wansford, on the delightful Nene Valley Railway, is the setting for No. 66718 on 19 June during a driver training run to Peterborough - note the new Metronet branded JNA wagons. *(John Rudd*

(Bottom Right) : Venturing onto Southern metals, 'Metronet' No. 66718 passes Addlestone Moor on the outskirts of Chertsey on 25 August with 4Y19, Mountfield - Southampton Western Docks Gypsum empties. There is little doubt the Metronet livery is aesthetically pleasing! *(Chris Nevard*

Midland Miscellany

(Above) : I/C BSO 9526 replaces DVT 82131 after it fails and Virgin Cross Country revert to locomotive haulage in Top and tail mode for almost 2 weeks. Class 90s Nos. 90034 and 90018 pass Levenshulme on 7 April with the 10:24 Manchester Piccadilly - Birmingham New Street.   *(Alan Sherratt)*

(Below) : From 10 April, 4L46, Ditton - Purfleet intermodal goes over to DRS Class 37/6 traction as a consequence of DRS hiring Class 66s out to Freightliner. On 11 May, Nos. 37069 + 37059 enter Tamworth Low level station with 4L46; a service to be axed later in the year as a result of poor loadings. *(Martin Buck)*

Scottish Miscellany

(Above) : As in 2005, the Edinburgh 'Binliner' is regularly hauled by a Class 37 in 2006 but, on 4 April, Class 60 No. 60075 is unusually diagrammed to work the train, seen at Dolphingston, on the Prestonpans diversion, with 6B44, Oxwellmains - Powderhall empties.
(Chris Perkins)

(Middle) : Three days later and Class 37/4 No. 37416 is rostered to work 6G90, 15:30 Millerhill - Ayr Falkland Junction MGR empties, seen powering away from Slateford Jct. and through Slateford station.
(Chris Perkins)

(Right) : For a Mills Hill - Perth excursion on 22 April, Class 47/8s Nos. 47826 and 47851 are rostered to work in top and tail mode. The Inter-City liveried example is in good form as it powers the train along the Edinburgh & Glasgow main line at Gogar on the western outskirts of Scotland's capital city
(Peter Kellett)

Southern Miscellany

(Above) : Staple motive power on the Basingstoke line is 'Sheds' and 'Freds' and Freightliner's Class 47/8 No. 47841 (still sporting Virgin red livery) is a most welcome sight at Worting Junction on 3 April dragging Wessex unit 2405 on 5X43, Bournemouth - Ilford EMD.   *(Chris Perkins)*

(Below) : The following day, Class 67s Nos. 67019 & 67013 working in 'Top 'n' tail' formation pass through St. Denys on a Bournemouth - Salisbury Serco test train. The line to Fareham and Portsmouth Harbour can be seen leading away to the right.   *(Nick Joynson)*

Western Miscellany

(Above) : A pair of 'Peds' working in Top 'n' tail formation (Nos. 31601 *The Mayor of Casterbridge* and No. 31285) make their way up the famous Lickey Incline near Finstall while working 1Z06, Worcester - Derby RTC test train on 6 April - note the contrasting livery carried by each locomotive.   *(Don Gatehouse)*

(Below) : Picturesque Dolau station on the Heart of Wales line is the setting for No. 47714 in Anglia livery + No. 47818 in One livery heading 10 coaches and DVT No. 82134 on the end, which form 1Z63, 06:05 Preston - Cardiff Compass Railtour on 29 April.   *(Adrian Kenny)*

Forders Virtual Quarry

After two years of being a 'virtual' Virtual Quarry (i.e. mothballed!), Forders VQ has finally been brought into use, as a replacement for Rugby VQ, which closed at the end of March to enable realignment work to take place north of Rugby station as part of the WCML upgrade. Up to three daily trains serve the new facility, all run by EWS, except those marked * which are operated by Freightliner, thus:

arrivals

7B42,	07:00 (SX)	Toton - Forders
		(arrive 10:00)
6A15,	05:25 (SO)	Bescot - Forders
		(arrive 10:00)
6A15,	10:02 (MSX)	Bescot - Forders
		(arrive 16:27)
6A10*,	16:05 (FX)	Stud Farm - Forders
		(arrive 18:35)

departures

6F12*,	09:10 (MX)	Forders - Stud Farm
6G15,	09:30 (SX)	Forders - Bescot
6D42,	12:12 (SX)	Forders - Toton

(Above) : On the Midland Mainline, Class 66/5 No. 66523 heads one of the Freightliner operated trains passing the old steam shed at Wellingborough on 18 July. The working is 6A10, Stud Farm - Forders VQ formed entirely of a uniform rake of loaded ballast wagons, which is in complete contrast to the photograph below. Note, the four wind turbines in the distance. *(John Rudd)*

(Below) : Trundling along the 'Up Slow' line at Oakley, Class 66/0 No. 66184 heads 7B42, Toton - Forders civil trip with a varied consist - note, in particular, the 1950's 'Shark' ballast plough brake vans. *(Nigel Gibbs)*

37669 / 37670

(Above) : EWS shuffle the Class 37 fleet again and reinstate, albeit briefly, Class 37/5 Nos. 37669 from Bescot and No. 37670 *St Blazey T&RS Depot* from Temple Mills. On 4 April, the pair are seen in a cutting climbing away from Chepstow with 6M41, Margam - Round Oak. *(Peter Slater)*

(Below) : On 10 April the pair are rostered to work 7C79, 12:45 East Usk (ex-Parc Slip) - Westbury Cement Works, seen leaving East Usk with a rake of 36 loaded HAA/HDA/HMA wagons - the pair return on 7C79, Westbury - Parc Slip and into storage! *(Adrian Kenny)*

'G & SW' Diversions

The Easter weekend sees the closure of The 'Caley' from Gretna Junction to Carstairs, resulting in a reduced Virgin West Coast/Cross Country service diverted via the Glasgow & South Western route through Kilmarnock and Dumfries - the diversions also include a limited number of freights.

(Top Left) : Class 66/4 No. 66404 passes the former opencast mining site at Gateside with the lightly loaded 4M44, Coatbridge - Daventry.

(Middle) : Looking in the opposite direction under a threatening sky, Class 60 No. 60075 heads 6S36, Dalston - Grangemouth empty bogie tanks, consisting of 18 TEA's.

(Below) : The month of April also sees the first Pendolino to be 'dragged' over the route when a trial run takes place on 4 April. However, it is not long before scheduled Pendolino services appear on the route, such as during the Easter Weekend. The first northbound passenger diversion is 1S44, Euston - Glasgow seen passing Kirkconnel hauled by Thunderbird Class 57/3 No. 5730 *Gordon Tracy*. (All Peter Kellet)

Cambrian 'Firsts'

(Right) : The first railtour of 2006 to visit the Cambrian Coast is the Kingfisher Railtours 'Snowdonia Explorer' excursion from Bedford to Pwllheli on 15 April. The Cambrian Coast line was governed in its construction by the frequent proximity of mountains and an encroaching coast as shown vividly in this view of Class 37/4 No. 37425 *Pride of the Valleys* heading the excursion on the approach to Llanaber. *(Julie Gerrard)*

(Middle) : On 29 April, a Class 33 locomotive visits the Cambrian Coast Line line on passenger duties, reportedly a first for the Class. The occasion is Pathfinder Tours 'Cambrian Borderer' excursion from Taunton to Barmouth featuring FM Rail's Class 33/1 No. 33103 *Swordfish* and Class 33/2 No. 33202 *Meteor*. The leading loco, No. 33103, crosses Borthwen Viaduct (if such a structure can be called a viaduct!) on the approach to Barmouth with the the outward leg of the tour. *(Nick Gerrard)*

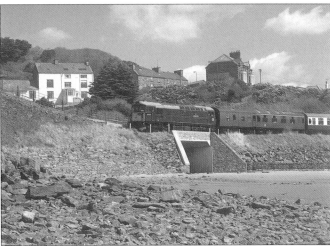

(Below) : At the destination, No. 33202 is pictured at Barmouth on the rear of the train, pending the return journey to Taunton. *(Julie Gerrard)*

Blue Pullman - Highland Bound ....

(Above) : On Good Friday, 14 April, The Blue Pullman sets off from King's Cross for a weekend's tour north of the border. The train's locomotives (Nos. 47709 *Dyonisos* and 47712 *Artemis*) had earlier moved light to Edinburgh along with No. 47703 *Hermes*, included for insurance! The train is seen passing Blindwells, a former open cast coal loading point, on the approach to Edinburgh hauled by Class 87 No. 87006.

(Below) : In the early evening, the train continues its journey to Inverness, via The Forth Bridge, seen here with the Nanking Blue 47s at the head, high above North Queensferry.

(Above) : After two days touring the Far North and Kyle lines, the train returns south from Inverness and the insurance policy reaps dividends as No. 47709 fails! At the highest point of the journey, and for that matter the highest point on the rail network some 1,484 feet above sea level, Druimauchdar was crested during heavy rain which hid the snow covered gullies of the surrounding Bens, with No. 47703 leading the defective No. 47709 on the front of the train and No. 47712 attached to the rear.

(Below) : After a pathing stop at Blair Atholl, the ensemble continue south alongside the River Tay near Dalguise, as the trees await the arrival of their summer foliage and the river takes the melting snow waters down to the sea - a truly Scottish spring scene for a truly magnificent train! *(All Peter Kellett)*

FHH Hire in DRS 66/4s

Having gained new freight traffic from EWS, Freightliner do not have a sufficient number of their own locomotives to cover all of the daily freight duties.

Consequently, there is no option but to hire in additional motive power from other operators and Freightliner hire in two Class 66/4 locomotives from Direct Rail Services:-

No. 66407   No. 66409

(Top Right) : One of Freightliner's Bardon Hill aggregate gains from EWS (6M79, Angerstein Wharf - Bardon Hill) passes Oakley on the Midland Mainline near Bedford on 30 May with hired Class 66/4 No. 66407 hauling a rake of empty JGA stone hoppers.   *(Nigel Gibbs)*

(Top Left) : On 23 April, 'Dred' No. 66409 is called upon to work 6C51, 18:23 Redcar - West Burton power station loaded HHAs, seen at South Bank, Teesside.   *(Ian Ball)*

(Bottom Left) : Initially, the hired-in locomotives find work on coal trains, such as 6M51, 12:37 Hull Docks - Rugeley power station, which is seen passing Hessle (Hull) on 14 April with No. 66409 in charge. The mainline runs parallel to the A63 road at this point with Hessle station also in view.   *(Robert France)*

(Below) : On 8 August, No. 66407 finds itself powering 4V60, Calvert - Bath/Bristol 'Binliner', passing Steventon, just west of Didcot.   *(Chris Nevard)*

Buncefield Legacy

The disastrous fire at the Buncefield Oil Storage Depot on 11 December 2005 is causing supply problems, so much so that oil trains from Lindsey Refinery to Colnbrook and/or Theale are having to run on a daily basis.

(Above) : Class 60 No. 60002 *High Peak* passes Woodley Green, Twyford with one of these additional services - 6Z79, Didcot Yard (ex-Lindsey) - Colnbrook loaded petroleum tanks. *(Ian Ball)*

FGW HST Upgrade

First Group expand its Great Western operation to include Wessex Trains, Thameslink and West Anglia & Great Northern routes under the First Capital Connect brand. To mark the launch, the Company unveil their 'neon' livery (officially known as 'dynamic lights') powered by MTU engined Nos. 43004 and 43009.

(Middle) : 'Neon' liveried HST power car No. 43009 at Cardiff Central.

(Left) : As further MTU repowering takes place, power cars will appear in a plain blue livery, minus 'Neon' branding, as carried by No. 43175 at Newport station. *(Both Martin Buck)*

Griffin Wharf Revival

The branch from Halifax Junction south of Ipswich Tunnel to Griffin Wharf, on the banks of the River Orwell, reopens to freight traffic after being out of use for five years. The branch will serve the ABP Port of Ipswich West Bank terminal handling aggregate traffic of sea-dredged sand and gravel.

(Above) : A test train runs on 25 April comprising 20 MEA box wagons hauled by Class 66/0 No. 66150, but the first booked working doesn't run until 11 May when No. 66046 works 6Z25, 08:45 Parkeston Quay - Ipswich Griffin Wharf, seen upon arrival at the terminal. *(Iain Scotchman)*

'S. & C.' Divert

(Below) : On 29 April, engineering work on the northern stretch of the WCML between Preston and Carlisle results in services being diverted over the Settle & Carlisle, including 6S55, Burngullow - Irvine china clay tanks seen passing through Ribblehead station behind Class 66/0 No. 66212. *(Fred Kerr)*

Westbury Diversions

(Above) : For five Saturdays, commencing 29 April, freightliner traffic to/from Southampton is diverted from the normal route due to resignalling in the Basingstoke area. Instead, the trains are routed from Didcot via Swindon, Thingley Junction and Westbury. On the first Saturday of diversions, No. 66503 passes Hawkeridge Junction, just east of Westbury, hauling 4O54, Leeds - Southampton.

(Below) : Meanwhile, the 4O02, (SO) Lawley Street - Southampton 'liner' is booked a Class 66/57 combination as proven in this view of No. 66505 + No. 57002 F*reightliner Phoenix* passing a rake of JHA hoppers stabled in front of Westbury Signalling Centre.

(Above) : Freight traffic on the Great Western mainline in the 'Up' direction between Bristol and Wootton Bassett Junction is restricted to 7B12, Merehead - Wootton Bassett stone train, so the diverted 4M55, Southampton - Lawley Street freightliner is a photographic opportunity not to be missed. With favourable sunny conditions on 20 May, Class 66/5 No. 66577 makes light work hauling 4M55 up the '1 in 100' gradient of Dauntsey Bank with a rake of empty KTA/FEA container flats.

(Below) : On the same day, No. 66542 leaves the GWML behind to begin the journey along the single line section from Thingley Junction to Bradford Junction with the diverted and fully laden 4O27, Ditton - Southampton freightliner. *(All Martin Buck)*

Intermodal Upheaval - New Kid on the Block

a) First the bad news - DRS abandon it's lightly-loaded Ditton - Purfleet chemical service, in favour of Anglo-Scottish traffic for Russells, which has been won from EWS. Two trains a day run in each direction, as follows:

4Z39, 05:00 (SX) Coatbridge - Daventry	4Z40, 18:38 (SX) Daventry - Coatbridge
4M48, 19:02 (SX) Coatbridge - Daventry	4S63, 06:31 (SX) Daventry - Coatbridge

These services directly replace 4M41/4S46/4M38/4S62, which no longer run.

b) The good news is a new player enters the railfreight market - *fastline*, a subsidiary of Jarvis, who start running a new intermodal service from between Thamesport (Grain) and Doncaster Railport (Birch Coppice as well later in the year). The first scheduled train runs on 8 May.

4O90, 11:01 (MWFO) Doncaster - Thamesport

4E90, 00:05 (TThSO) Thamesport - Doncaster

Due to pathing restrictions, the train is routed in both directions via Chesterfield, Tamworth and the Sutton Park Line to Bescot, thence down the WCML to London, calling at Rugby for a crew change.

Motive power is in the shape of three refurbished Class 56 locomotives (No. 56301/2/3) bringing the sight of classic traction back to the mainline after a two-year absence - great news for the enthusiast!

Fastline 'Grid'

(Left) : The new fastline logo, which will appear on the side panels of the Company's fleet of 'Grids'. To facilitate the new service, Fastline have their own set of new FEA-B container flats (Nos. 643001 - 643024), which are semi-permanently coupled in pairs. *(Martin Buck)*

(Below) : The choice of Rugby for 4O90 to change crew is the ideal location for rail enthusiasts to observe the locomotive and consist in great detail, such as in this close up view of No. 56301 awaiting departure time on the 'up' goods line. *(Martin Buck)*

(Above) : The originating point for the initial Southbound service will be Doncaster Belmont Yard, where Class 56/3 No. 56301 waits to leave on 17 July with 4O90 bound for Thamesport. *(John Rudd)*

(Below) : A healthier payload is visible on 28 June when No. 56302 trundles through the urban landscape of Inner London (White City, in fact) with 4O90, Doncaster - Thamesport. *(Marc Ely)*

Southern Serco

(Above) : With effect from May, 'Heritage' traction gains new work when FM Rail replace EWS as traction provider for the southern Serco test train contract using Class 47 locomotives No. 47145 *Myrrdin Emrys* and No. 47355 *Avocet.* On 2 May, Class 47/3 No. 47355 Top 'n' tails Class 47/0 No. 47145 on 1Z14, 07:52 Derby RTC - Acton Canal Wharf heading south past Oakley on the Midland Mainline.   *(Nigel Gibbs)*

(Below) : The ex-Tinsley flagship loco. No. 47145 passes Loughor to the west of Swansea, where the A484 runs parallel to the mainline, with a rearranged 1Z14, 09:30 Fishguard Harbour - Swansea Serco test train on 8 June. The train being re-scheduled following a failure at Fishguard the day before. Note that both locos. are providing power in multiple.   *(Mark Thomas)*

New Scottish Charter Season

(Above) : For the opening 'Royal Scotsman' of the season, Class 47/8 No. 47854 is very well prepared, but the star of the show is Class 37/0 No. 37214. Resplendent in a new coat of paint, she is seen attached to the rear of the train as two passengers stand on the veranda of the former Pullman coach as they depart the western suburbs of Edinburgh on 6 May. *(Peter Kellett)*

(Below) : The SRPS rail tour season gets into full swing on 6 May with a North Berwick - Mallaig excursion using Class 47's (Nos. 47245 and 47851 *Traction Magazine*) in Top 'n' tail mode. A weather stained No. 47851 brings up the rear as the train breasts County March Summit with the magnificent sight of Ben Dorain towering 3,523 feet dominating the skyline . Two West Highland Way walkers turn and see one mindless gentleman 'flayling' from a first coach window! *(Peter Kellett)*

Welsh Specials

Bristol East 'Pride'

(Left) : On 4 May, 'Control' turn out Class 37/4 No. 37425 *Pride of the Valleys* on 6C01, Newport ADJ - Bristol East Depot steel train which is seen storming up the incline past Cattybrook brickworks, near Almondsbury, on the western outskirts of Bristol. *(Chris Perkins)*

New   'Dreds'

(Middle) : On a dreadfully dreary day, following their unloading at Newport Docks, three new DRS Class 66/4's Nos. 66411, 66412 and 66413 (nearest) are towed away by No. 66403. The cavalcade heads along the branch on 30 May towards ADJ yard, running as 0Z66 15:00 Newport Docks - Carlisle Kingmoor.
(Adrian Kenny)

MoD Manoeuvre

(Below) : 'One off' Ministry of Defence workings are always worth a photograph, despite the weather, as the consist is usually interesting. As the gloom descends, Class 66/0 No. 66098 passes Llandeilo Junction on 26 May with a rake of 12 KWA Warwells forming 7X40, 17:39 Haverfordwest - Didcot Yard.
(Mark Thomas)

FA Cup Final - 13 May

(Above) : For this sporting spectacular, several relief trains are laid on to facilitate the increase in passengers visiting the Principality, such as 2N94, 13:35 Cardiff Central - Newport seen passing Newport ADJ Yard hauled by heritage Class 50 No. 50031 *Hood* . *(Mark Thomas)*

Football League Division 1 Play Off Final - 27 May

(Below) : Having lost to Barnsley after extra time on penalties, Swansea fans journey home behind Class 37/4 No. 37425 *Pride of the Valleys* working top 'n' tail with Class 50 No 50031 *Hood* on 1Z39, 17:30 Cardiff - Swansea. After setting down passengers, the ensemble leaves as 5Z40, 18:25 Swansea - Cardiff ECS; giving the first 37 and a 50 on a passenger train into Swansea for many years. *(Adrian Kenny)*

Tees Freightliner

(Above) : On 4 May, Class 66/5 No. 66532 fails on 4L79, Wilton - Felixstowe near Bowesfield Junction and is dragged back to Tees Yard by an EWS Class 60. Another Class 66/5 (No. 66526) is sent to collect the train and proceed - the first time Freightliner have been allowed to use Tees Yard as EWS own it. *(Ian Ball)*

Motorail Axe

FGW take the decision to axe the West of England Motorail service this summer, which has been made in connection with the reprieve of the Penzance sleeper and the Company's evaluation of costs. Basically, the use of the fleet of car carriers (Nos. 96602 - 96609) could not be justified, which are only used for a handful of weekends in the year.

(Below) : On 4 May, the eight redundant Motorail vans pass through Pangbourne en-route from Old Oak Common to Long Marston for storage, hauled by Class 66/0 No. 66229. As one can see, creeping foliage is beginning to make this location a less attractive proposition for railway photography. *(Nic Joynson)*

Fife Coal

(Above) : One of the most interesting, but seldom photographed, areas of the Scottish freight scene is the coal operations in Fife, featured here to put it on the map, so to speak! During May, Fergussons cease loading coal at Inverkeithing to consolidate operations at Thornton Yard and Class 66/0 No. 66121 is seen at the loading point in Inverkeithing Yard with 6G08, 15:55 departure to Drax. *(Don Gatehouse)*

(Below) : Westfield coal disposal point is situated at the end of a 4-mile single line spur, which leaves the Cowdenbeath Line at Redford Junction. There are several good vantage points to observe MGR services on the branch, such as Kinglassie where Class 66/0 No. 66126 passes with 7G31, 08:42 Westfield - Millerhill loaded MGR on 11 May. Coal trains from Westfield run to Millerhill, where they will be staged, pending onward movement to a receiving power station, like Cockenzie, for example. *(Don Gatehouse)*

Sleeper Sunset

Possibly the biggest passenger news in June is the end of Class 37s on the West Hihgland Line portion off the Caledonian sleeper. Effective June 10th, the much-loved 37/4s will be replaced by Class 67 locomotives. The first train to be worked by the new order is 1Y11, 04:50 Edinburgh Waverley - Fort William hauled by 'Skip' No. 67008. As a final tribute to the passing of 37s on this train, a couple of images are reproduced here.

(Above) : **The sun rises at 05:17 on the morning of 7 June as No.37405 crosses Linlithgow Viaduct with 1Y11, 04:50 Edinburgh Waverley - Fort William sleeper. However, the sun will set two days later on this period of railway operations when much vaunted 'Improvements' to the service will be introduced with the introduction of Class 67 power, and an additional nine minutes journey time!** *(Peter Kellett)*

(Below) : **On 11 May, No. 37406** *The Saltire Society* **passes over Garbh Ghoair viaduct on the approach to Rannoch station with 1Y11 sleeper portion.** *(Adrian Kenny)*

ATW Fishguard 50

Having already re-instated a morning and evening peak loco-hauled service on the Rhymney branch, due to a shortage of DMUs, Arriva Trains Wales have to bring in another diesel and coaches formation, this time to work the Summer Fishguard Harbour service.

(Top Right) : The outward service runs as 1B96, 10:55 Cardiff Central - Fishguard Harbour, which is seen at the outset of its journey in the care of Class 50 No. 50031 *Hood*. Note, the bodyside in view sports 50028 *Tiger* and a somewhat inappropriate Highland Rail Stag emblem!   *(Martin Buck)*

(Right) : The new service affords many good photographic opportunities, such as St. Ishmael where the railway skirts the River Tywi estuary; No. 50049 *Defiance* passes with 1B97, 13:35 Fishguard Harbour - Cardiff Central on 15 July.
              (Mark Thomas)

(Below) : Same loco., same train, but this time passing Margam Moors on 26 August, with the 'Hoover' still sporting *Benbow* nameplates from when it was No. 50012.   *(Adrian Kenny)*

VWC Electric

From the start of the Summer Timetable on 12 June, Virgin West Coast officially re-introduce a daily Class 87 diagram on the WCML to cover the withdrawal of Pendolino units for modification. After working an early morning Rugby - Euston service, the set lays over in London before making an evening return trip to Birmingham New Street.

(Above) : Class 87 No. 87002 *The AC Locomotive Group,* in the striking purple Porterbrook livery, waits to leave Euston on 11 July with 1G21, the 16:51 service to Birmingham. *(Iain Scotchman)*

(Below) : Sporting St. George cross-style buffers, applied by Wembley Depot staff to mark England's participation in the FIFA 2006 World Cup, No. 87006 is an impressive sight passing Dudswell on 15 June with 1G21, 16:51 Euston - Birmingham New Street. *(Nic Joynson)*

Rylestone Stone

GBRf gain a short term contract (eight weeks) to move stone from Swinden Quarry, near Skipton on the Rylestone Branch, to Bury St. Edmunds in connection with construction work at Stansted Airport.

6L45, 08:47 (MWO) Rylestone - Bury St. Edmunds   6E14, 15:09 (TThO) Bury St. Edmunds - Rylestone

(Above) : **A delightful rural setting for Class 66/7 No. 66719 heading down the Rylestone Branch on 5 June with 6L45, Rylestone - Bury St. Edmunds loaded JNA wagons; one load of a reported 40,000 tonnes of stone scheduled to be moved. The trains are routed via Calder Bridge Junction, Doncaster, Peterborough and Ely and will prove a magnet for photographers of the new 'Metronet' Class 66/7's.** *(Fred Kerr)*

Ayr Cement

Above) : **Oxwellmains despatches cement to Aberdeen, Brunthill, Inverness, Seaham, Viewpark and now a new weekly flow to Ayr Harbour. Class 66/6 No. 66617 awaits departure at Ayr Harbour on 19 June with 6Z95, 16:24 Ayr Harbour - Oxwellmains cement empties.** *(Don Gatehouse)*

Esk Invader

(Above) : The CFPS 'Whistler', Class 40 No. 40145, storms past Welbeck Disposal Point, Goose Hill, on 3 June heading for the North Yorkshire coast with 1Z40, 06:37 Crewe - Whitby charter. *(Ian Ball)*

North Downs 'Belle'

(Below) : On the same day, a Northern Belle excursion to Reigate provides the unusual sight of a diesel locomotive-hauled passenger train on the North Downs Line; railtour traffic is predominantly steam-hauled. 'Silver Skip' No. 67029 leads the return 1Z83, 19:10 Reigate - London Victoria past Shalford Junction in glorious light bound for Woking and Staines - No. 67012 being on the rear. *(Marc Ely)*

West Coast 47s

(Above) : Railtours are often the high points in any season, and to be lucky enough to capture them in bright sunshine is always a bonus. Double-headed Nos. 47813 and 47714 return such a tour from Carlisle on 3 June at Great Strickland comprising of a former Virgin set of MkIII's complete with DVT plus a former First GW MkIII sleeper. *(Peter Kellett)*

(Below) : Seven days later and what a day, bright sun and clear sky from the word go! A good old reliable SRPS Railtour using West Coast Railways Class 47s is caught on film working an excursion from Glenrothes to Chester featuring Nos. 47245 topping and 47851 tailing. The ensemble is at Littlegill in the Upper Clyde Valley approaching a pathing stop in Abington 'Up' loop. *(Peter Kellett)*

South West Turns

(Above) : Loco-hauled activity in Devon and Cornwall has significantly reduced in volume over the last few years, not helped of course by the loss of Royal Mail trains and loco-hauled VXC services. For the rail enthusiast, variety is to be found more and more with 'specials' and one-off workings. On 1 June, after taking the Queen to St. Austell, Class 67s Nos. 67006 *Royal Sovereign* and 67005 *Queen's Messenger* pass the site of Silverton station, top 'n' tailing 5Z58, 10:18 St. Austell - Wolverton ECS. *(Dave Mitchell)*

(Below) : GBRf locomotives are not particularly common in the south west of England, so there is a bonus when a pair of Class 66/7s, Nos. 66715 *Valour....* and 66703 *Doncaster PSB 1981-2002,* work 6G50, 16:30 Westbury - Par rail train on 4 June, seen passing Exminster. *(Dave Mitchell)*

The 'Orcadian'

(Above) : To Scotland in style .... for a luxury weekend outing to the Far North and Kyle lines. Motive power is in the shape of former mainline favourites Nos. 50031 *Hood* and 50049 *Defiance* running in the guise of 50028 *Tiger* and 50012 *Benbow* on one side only. The pair are seen passing Stoke Prior on 16 June working the outward leg of the tour - 1Z27, 06:40 Swindon - Inverness. *(Don Gatehouse)*

The Last Post

(Below) : The sole remaining ReS-liveried Class 90 in service with 'ONE' is No. 90019 *Penny Black* seen passing Brantham on 29 June with 1P27, 10:30 Norwich - Liverpool Street. *(Andy Small)*

'LT & S' PULLMAN

(Above) : The Blue Pullman makes its revenue-earning debut on the London, Tilbury & Southend route, operating an afternoon and evening trip from London to Essex on 28 June . No. 47709 *Dionysos* leads the first train of the day (1Z47, 12:15 Fenchurch Street - Shoeburyness) past Shadwell with No. 47712 *Artemis* on the rear. The Swiss Re Tower, better known as 'The Gherkin', dominates the skyline.   *(Marc Ely)*

(Below) : In Mediterranean conditions, No. 47712 *Artemis* leads as the train skirts the Essex coastline at Chalkwell with the return leg of the first trip - 1Z48, 13:54 Shoeburyness - Fenchurch Street.   *(Marc Ely)*

JULY

Cars Restart

After a trial period earlier in the year, EWS recommence running loaded car trains from Southampton Western Docks:

6Z16, 02:30 (TWFO) Washwood Heath - Southampton W. D.

6Z23, 14:10 (TWFO) Southampton W. D. - Bescot

To enable the vehicles to remain the 'right way round', 6Z23 is routed via Redbridge, Romsey, the Laverstock loop and Andover. From Birmingham, the vehicles are conveyed to their final destinations by existing automotive/Enterprise services.

(Right) : **The new 6Z23, 13:10 Southampton Western Docks - Bescot, hauled by Class 66/0 No. 66049, passes Hatton North Junction conveying Ford vans, using both IFA and IPA wagons.** *(Peter Tandy)*

(Below) : **The same service is seen again on 8 August hauled by No. 66183 climbing up the grade past Cholsey Manor Farm.** *(Chris Nevard)*

Last Olympian ....

(Left) : Not to be outdone, although Scotland did not participate in the World Cup, the buffers on Class 87 No. 87012 *The Olympian* are adorned with the Saint Andrew's cross for its visit north of the border on 30 June to collect defective Class 325 unit No. 325005 from Polmadie. On the Monday, the 87, complete with a spaceman attached to the handrail, passes Cartland, north of Lanark Junction, on reportedly its last journey from Glasgow, hauling the defective mail unit. *(Peter Kellett)*

Drax Lime

Freightliner *Heavy Haul* continue to expand their share of the Peak Forest aggregates market .... whilst already operating limestone trains from Dowlow to Cottam and Eggborough, Tunstead to Ratcliffe and West Burton another new flow now starts running to Drax:

6Z56, 06:40 (FX) Tunstead - Drax   6Z96, 12:20 (FX) Drax - Tunstead

(Below) : Running some 3 hours late, Class 66/6 No. 66609 makes for a fine sight passing Edale on 14 July with 6Z56, 06:40 Tunstead - Drax loaded limestone bogie hoppers   *(Alan Hazelden)*

Yarmouth '*Drags*'

(Above) : Railway photographers, seeking out loco-hauled passenger activity, flock to the Great Yarmouth line on Summer Saturdays to record the 'Drags'. On 7 July, Class 47/7 No. 47714 with 'One-liveried' Class No. 90009 DIT passes Reedham Junction with 1V18, 10:00 Liverpool St.- Gt.Yarmouth.   *(Iain Scotchman)*

(Below) : A typical scene on Saturday, 15 July, and Class 47/8 No. 47810 *Porterbrook* waiting to leave Great Yarmouth with DBSO 9709 + Class 90 No. 90019 Penny Black on the rear of 5V26, 15.35 empty coaching stock to Norwich Crown Point.   *(Iain Scotchman)*

NMT HST Substitute

Instrumentation problems with the New Measurement Train (NMT) during July (and into the autumn!) results in Network Rail using a scratch set of test vehicles centred around the high speed track recording coach No. 99550 with a pair of DRS Class 37/6s providing the power, working in top 'n' tail formation. The train formation comprises:

- Support Coach/Runner No. DB 977986   - Mk 2f Track recording Coach No. 999550
- Support Coach/Dormitory No. DB977337   - Generator Coach No. 6264

The set will find itself during the summer months working throughout the network until the HST is once again ready for use and provides the rare sight of DRS traction on routes not normally associated with the Class. A couple of images are included which feature the substitute NMT working on ex-Great Western metals; a Friday's Only service, which works to a two-week diagram, taking in the GWML via Swindon one week, followed by the 'Berks. & Hants.' via Westbury, the next.

(Left) : The author's first sighting of this train takes place on 28 July when Nos. 37607 + 37612 pass Wootton Bassett Junction top 'n' tailing 1A01, 09:12 Taunton - Swindon Cocklebury. *(Martin Buck)*

(Below) : Later that day, the elevated section of the A48 road at Briton Ferry provides an excellent vantage point to view the pair working 1Z94, 15:01 Swansea - Derby Etches Park. Meanwhile, Class 50 No. 50031 *Hood* waits to leave the Swansea District Line with 1B97, 13:35 Fishguard Harbour - Cardiff Central. A rake of MEA wagons are stabled in the yard and the line in the left foreground leads to Baglan Bay. *(Mark Thomas)*

More Scrap ....

Another freight gain for Freightliner *Heavy Haul* in July is 'new to rail' scrap metal traffic from Hitchin to both Cardiff and Sheerness:

6Z92, 03:00 (MO) Hitchin - Cardiff	6Z93, 05:50 (ThO) Cardiff - Hitchin
6Z99, 19:10 (ThO) Hitchin - Sheerness	6Z77, 03:20 (SO) Sheerness - Hitchin

The following month sees a further new flow of scrap metal from the East Midlands scrapyard at Beeston to Hull King George Dock for export using JNA wagons. The outward service is routed via Chesterfield, the 'Old Road', Doncaster and Selby whilst the 'empties' go via Selby, Doncaster, Gainsborough and Newark Castle on the return journey.

6Z90, 12:10 (MWFO) Beeston - Hull	6Z91, 06:30 (TThSO) Hull - Beeston

(Right) : A rake of box wagons come out of storage for the Hitchin flow and on 22 June Class 66/6 No. 66606 passes Lower Moor heading 6Z71, 11:29 Long Marston - Hitchin; the first time a Class 66/6 locomotive uses this stretch of the Cotswold Line. *(Peter Tandy)*

(Below) : Class 66/5 No. 66561 hurries along the 'Down' goods line at Chesterfield on 14 August with 6Z90, 14:38 Beeston - Hull King George Dock loaded scrap. In the background, No. 66501 'Japan 2001' slows for a signal check with 4E44, Southampton-Leeds freightliner. *(John Binch)*

Off The Beaten Track

(Above) : If it wasn't for sign, would you recognise Sudbury? Situated at the end of a single track branch line off the Great Eastern Mainline at Marks Tey. Class 31/1 No. 31128 *Charybdis* sits at the rear of 1Z47 05:25 NENTA "North Countryman" Railtour to Newcastle on 15 July.   *(Iain Scotchman)*

(Below) : Stamford, Lincolnshire, and Class 37/0 No. 37218   trundling through the station with the Stoneblower on 11 July, running as 6Z37, Nottingham - Ashford.   *(John Rudd)*

Leven Viaduct Re-opens

On Monday, 17 July, at 05:00 hours rail services start running across Leven Viaduct in south Cumbria again, following 16 weeks of refurbishment work. The first passenger train crosses the viaduct shortly after 5am. The completion (on schedule!) of this £14 million project by Network Rail will mean smoother and quieter rides for passengers as they cross the viaduct. It also means no further major maintenance work will be required on the viaduct for at least 25 years.

(Above) : **The following day, 18 July, DRS Class 20/3s Nos. 20313 + 20312 cross Leven Viaduct, Ulverston, with the weekly 6C27, Sandbach - Sellafield acid tank train. Note, some piers still need their stonework grouted and staging is still in place for this work.** *(Andrew Naylor)*

(Below) : **Whilst this work was being carried out, services normally using the Cumbrian Coast route were diverted via Carlisle and Shap, such as 6C52, Heysham - Sellafield flasks seen passing through the cutting at Shap Summit on 10 May, headed by DRS locomotives Nos. 37605 + No. 20306.** *(Robert France)*

New TEA Bogie Tanks

July sees the arrival of new 100-tonne TEA bogie petroleum tank wagons; VTG for Murco services (Port Clarence and Robeston refineries) along with EWS tank wagons (Lindsey refinery). Built by Greenbrier Europe in Poland, both wagons are pretty well identical in design and will gradually replace the older TDA/TEA tank wagons on the respective circuits, some of which date back to the 1960s.

(Above) : The new EWS tankers are moved to Humberside in the consist of '*Enterprise*' working 6X77, Wembley - Mossend. Here, the service passes Carpenders Park on 20 July hauled by Class 92 No. 92005 *Mozart* with the tankers conveniently situated at the front of the train. *(Nic Joynson)*

(Top Left) :The first batch of VTG bogie tank wagons are moved to Robeston oil refinery on Monday, 24 July, almost a week later than originally booked, by FM Rail's No. 47703 *Hermes*. The colourful formation passes through Cardiff, running as 6Z59,11:00 Wembley - Robeston, with part of the Millennium Stadium visible on the left of picture. *(Adrian Kenny)*

(Bottom Left) : No. VTG 88130 at Swindon on Monday 24 July. *(Martin Buck)*

(Below) : No. EWS 870217 at Washwood Heath on 29 September. *(Martin Buck)*

Royal Welsh Show

(Above) : It is believed that ATW have a 3 year contract with the Class 50 Alliance to use their locos. for specials and reliefs, etc. On 25 July, Class 50 No. 50049 *Defiance* running in the guise of No. 50012 *Benbow* is turned out to work a Royal Welsh Show special, seen approaching Pantyffynnon with 1Z37, 07:28 Cardiff - Llandrindod Wells, running 43 minutes late. *(Mark Thomas)*

(Below) : The same train is seen again at Berthddu on the Heart of Wales Line with the '50' hauling six MkI vehicles; one in Virgin livery and five in the striking turquoise Arriva livery. *(Adrian Kenny)*

DRS Turns

(Right) : DRS locomotives are no longer restricted to freight duties as, for example, on 25 July when Class 47/5 No. 47501 passed Beck Houses with 1Z32, Carnforth - Carlisle DRS driver trainer. *(Alan Sherratt)*

(Below) : The Royal Scotsman requires a locomotive with Route Availability 5 capability to work the Oban line, but as West Coast Railway's own Class 37 is out of action for part of the summer, DRS Class 37/0 No. 37029 is hired-in. The locomotive starts up on   25 July for the short leg of the journey from Crianlarich to Taynuilt. *(Peter Kellett)*

FM Rail Coal

Seeking to attract freight customers, FM Rail run a trial coal working on behalf of UK Coal from Daw Mill Colliery to Rugeley Power Station. The trial utilises VTG-owned 2-axle aggregate hoppers and a trio of Class 31 locomotives, unusual traction due to the intended pair of slow-speed fitted Class 47s being unavailable. If successful, a short term contract to move 25,000 tonnes of coal to Rugeley could follow. If the trial proves a success, it could lead to FM Rail being awarded a six week long contract to move 25,000 tonnes of coal to Rugeley.

(Top Left) : In readiness for the trial, a rake of 60 PGA wagons move to Coalville. The train (6Z59, York - Coalville) is seen on 13 July at Monk Fryston with Class 47/0 No. 47145 *Myrrdin Emrys* in the process of crossing over from the 'Up' Normanton to the 'Up' Pontefract main line with its lengthy consist in tow.
(John Rudd)

(Bottom Left) : On 25 July, the trio of assorted liveried 'Goyles' Nos. 31190 *Gryphon* + 31601 + 31454 haul 6G20, 09:24 (rescheduled to 13:00) Daw Mill Colliery - Rugeley Power Station through Whitacre Junction; the train is heavily delayed through a late start from Mantle Lane (Coalville) and hot box problems on some of the PGA stock, all of which show as 'Cripples' on TRUST. *(Peter Tandy)*

EWS in France

EWS wish to expand into European operations and acquire an operating license for freight services in France. The Company is currently in the process of selecting and preparing up to 50 Class 66 locomotives for operation in France; one such locomotive is No. 66022, which initially travelled to France in June for trials with Euro Cargo Rail before returning to Toton (UK) in July for modifications and UIC-numbering, becoming GB 92. 70. 066000.-5, returning to France on 26 July.

(Above) : The *'French'* Class 66/0 No. 66022 is seen on the other side of the Channel stabled atop a rake of aggregate hoppers in the yard at Gravenchon Port Jérôme (near the River Seine) on 11 September having worked in from Calais (ex-Caffiers) via Amiens and Arras. The UIC number details appear below the cabside window and the 'Shed' sports a distinctive yellow & black striped snowplough. *(Laurent Charlier)*

Blue Pullman - A Final Look ....

(Above) : As the Blue Pullman continues to travel the length and breadth of the rail network, I indulge myself by taking a last look at this magnificent train in 2006 with four diverse views. On 1 July, Class 47/7 No. 47709 *Dyonisos,* with No. 47712 *Artemis* bringing up the rear, pass along the seafront at Dawlish with 1Z65, 07:15 Paddington - Paignton Blue Pullman.   *(Matt Turner)*

(Below) : Still with No. 47709 doing the work, the Blue Pullman leaves Keith on the single track Aberdeen - Inverness line on 8 July with 1Z21, Dumbarton - Inverness. Note the Chivas Brothers distillery bondhouse dominating the background.   *(Peter Kellett)*

(Above) : The Blue Pullman was booked to visit Stratford-upon-Avon on Saturday, 19 August, with a scheduled route via Hatton North Junction, but in the event it was diverted to run along the North Warwickshire Line via Henley-in-Arden. As usual, the train runs in 'top and tail' mode, but due to No. 47712 *Artemis* suffering a problem, Class 47/8 No. 47832 *Driver Tom Clark* has to run-round and take the train forward. *ANY* locomotive is exceptionally rare on this line and double-headed 47s totally unprecedented, seen heading 1Z53 ex- King's Cross passed the GWR signal box at Henley-in Arden.   *(Peter Tandy)*

(Below) : A dull day, but still worthwhile, to record the Blue Pullman on 26 August. Nos. 47712 and 47832 'top & tail' 1Z59, 07:30 Southend Central - York and away from the cameraman at Leigh-on-Sea, passing HMS Wilton, the headquarters of the Essex Yacht Club.   *(Iain Scotchman)*

ATW '57' Finishes (again!)

The Arriva Trains Wales Class 57 diagram runs for the final time on Tuesday, 1 August, after the return of Class 175 DMU No. 175103 to traffic following lengthy repairs.

The final day saw Class 57 No. 57315 *The Mole* appropriately work the diagram, as it was a regular sight on this service throughout the summer; a couple of views are reproduced, albeit with the same locomotive but on a different date!

(Top Left) : On 10 June, No. 57315 passes Daresbury, south of Warrington heading the 05:57 Holyhead - Manchester. *(Ian Ball)*

(Middle) : At the same location, but travelling in the opposite direction, No. 57315 works the next leg of the diagram, the 10:03 Manchester - Holyhead. *(Ian Ball)*

East Coast Tractor

(Below) : Class 37/4 No. 37405 is a surprise choice of traction to move redundant mail vans to Doncaster, seen passing Yaxley, Peterborough, on 4 August with 5Z27, Wembley - Doncaster. *(John Rudd)*

To the Rescue ....

(Above) : On 4 August, due to the non-availability of the 'booked' Class 66/4, a pair of Class 47/8s (Nos. 47815 + 47839) are hired-in to work 4M44, Mossend - Daventry intermodal and are seen passing Euxton on the northern section of the WCML with a partially loaded train of 'Malcolm' containers.   *(Fred Kerr)*

(Below) : After working north on 6S60, Class 66/7 No. 66708 fails and does not work back from Aberdeen on 4 August, so the operators hire in a FHH Class 66/6, which runs light engine from Oxwellmains to Aberdeen, to rescue the Bluebird. No. 66621 has charge of 6L59, Aberdeen - Harwich 'Mud Oil' empties with the disgraced No. 66708 hiding on the back, still inside North Queensferry tunnel.   *(Peter Kellett)*

Fishguard *100*

To celebrate 100 years of trains to the Port of Fishguard Harbour, Arriva Trains Wales operate a special train running as:

1Z50, 07:28 Tyseley - Fishguard Harbour   1Z51, 16:20 Fishguard Harbour - Tyseley

The trains will feature a combination of ex-Great Western Railway Castle Class 4-6-0 steam engine No. 5051 *Drysllwyn Castle* (later renamed *Earl Bathurst*) and Class 50 No. 50049 *Defiance*.

(Top Right) : The driver is ready for the off as No. 5051 prepares to leave Llanelli on 18 August with 1Z50 bound for Fishguard Harbour; the Class 50 will be attached to the train at Carmarthen.

(Bottom Right) : Steam appears to be emanating from pretty well everywhere as No. 5051 struggles up Cockett Bank, which has a ruling gradient of about 1 in 50, with 1Z51, the 16:20 ex-Fishguard charter returning to Tyseley, complete with a 'Red Dragon' headboard.   *(Both Mark Thomas)*

West Coast Duchess

(Below) : Pure unadulterated power. This striking view sees LMS 4-6-2 Stanier Pacific No. 6233 *Duchess of Sutherland* blasting out of Carnforth on 12 August 2006 with the ECS for Kingfisher's Dalesman tour from Hellifield to Carlisle and back. The train is running to Hellifield via Blackburn because of a ban on eastbound loco-hauled trains over the direct line from Carnforth to Settle Junction, caused by a weak bridge at Bentham. Other steam images in this title have been included to cover specific historical events, but I could not resist slipping this one in - I hope readers will not disapprove!   *(Andrew Naylor)*

SOUTHERN SPECIALS

'Schools Out'

(Left) : Class 66/0 No. 66138 drags Ex-Southern Railway steam locomotive No. E850 *Lord Nelson* through Romsey on 16 August from Eastleigh Works to the West Somerset Railway for running-in trials before use on mainline trips. The consist is Barriers Nos. 112153/110225/110771, 30850, - E850 - Support Coach No. 35317 and 112041/11070, respectively.

(Chris Perkins)

'Sunny Seaside Spitfire'

(Left) : On 17 August, a Kingfisher Railtours excursion runs in conjunction with the Eastbourne Air Show, bringing the extremely rare sight of an EWS Class 37/4 to the Sussex coast. The tour originates from Bristol Temple Meads and is routed via the GWML and Brighton main line to reach Sussex. Here No. 37405 approaches Hampden Park, some 2-miles out of Eastbourne, heading the return 1Z28, 17:12 Eastbourne - Bristol Temple Meads. *(Marc Ely)*

'Southern Belle'

(Left) : After decades as the staple traction in the south east, Class 33s are now relatively rare on their old stomping ground. On 23 September, No. 33025 becomes the first WCRC Crompton (and only the second WCRC loco) to reach Sussex, when it top 'n' tails the RTC's Southern Belle along with 'Battle of Britain' 4-6-2 pacific No. 34067 *Tangmere*. The train is seen on the approach to Littlehampton with the first leg of the return journey, 1Z83, 14:18 Bognor Regis - London Victoria. Apart from this 8.25 mile turning leg, 'Tangmere' headed the tour throughout. *(Marc Ely)*

SOME MORE SPECIALS

'Rutland Renegade'

(Right) : Perhaps, one of the railtours of the year takes place on 26 August when a trio of DRS Class 20/3 locomotives (Nos. 20306/309/314) are rostered to work 1Z81, the 07:58 Preston - Kettering. The trio are seen passing Kibworth on the Midland Mainline, some 17-miles from their destination.   (Nigel Gibbs)

Return of RSG

(Right) : The once familiar sight and sound of a Deltic storming along the ECML is resurrected on 29 August. Class 55 No. 55022 *Royal Scots Grey* makes a triumphant return to the main line in unison with No. 55002 *The King's Own Yorkshire Light Infantry* (Dead in Tow) + Class 47/7 No. 47703 *Hermes* . The train is passing Bolton Percy running as 5Z55, 10:10 Barrow Hill - York Holgate.   (Alan Sherratt)

'Vulture Squadron'

(Right) : An interesting choice of motive power! 'Metronet' Class 66/7 No. 66718 passes the old Esso fuel dump at Flax Bourton (mid-way between Parson Street and Nailsea & Blackwell) on 31 August with 5Z98, Laira - Derby stock move of ex-Virgin Mk3 coaches. The Class 66/7 arrived at Plymouth 'Dead-on-Rear' of the overnight 1C99 'Night Riviera' from London Paddington the previous day.
(Chris Perkins)

Wootton Bassett Blockade

For 5 days, commencing 25 August, a total engineering blockade of Wootton Bassett Junction comes into effect resulting in both passenger and freight services having to be diverted. As a general rule, South Wales services are routed via Gloucester and the Golden Valley to Swindon with Bristol services going via the 'Berks. & Hants.' therefore avoiding the blockaded area altogether.

(Above) : Although variable cloud rules out ideal weather for photography on each of the five days, two views are included for the record. Firstly, Class 66/5 No. 66515 hurries along the embankment above the Kennet & Avon Canal at Crofton on 29 August with 4V60, Calvert - Bath/Bristol empty 'Binliner'.

(Below) : Just under a mile further west on the same day, Class 60 No. 60038 *AvestaPolarit* passes a set of lock gates with 6B33, Theale - Robeston empty petroleum tanks.   *(Both Martin Buck)*

'Tesco Express'

Eddie Stobart, the well known road haulier, enters the railfreight market on 19 September, running trains for Tesco. DRS provide the traction and Class 66/4 No. 66411 is unveiled in a striking new livery named 'Eddie the Engine' .

The new service runs as:

4S43, 06:31 (SX)
Daventry - Grangemouth

4M48, 17:40 (SX)
Grangemouth - Daventry

The new service will use lowliner container flats carrying a total of twenty six 45ft. 'Curtainsiders', each displaying 'Stobart Rail' and Tesco's 'Less CO_2' branding.

As a consequence of this new service, the existing *Russell* intermodal train (4S44/4M62) is retimed.

(Below) : **The official launch day turns out to be a glorious late-summer's day with unbroken sunshine, as if proof was needed in this view. No. 66411 crosses the River Esk viaduct at Floriston, just under 7 miles out of Carlisle.**
(Robert France)

(Above) : **A close up of 'Eddie The Engine' passing Swynnerton (WCML) with the inaugural 4S43.** *(Mark Williams)*

(Below) : **A close up of a Tesco 'Less CO2' branded curtainsider passing Rugby on the first day of operations.** *(Martin Buck)*

Working of the Year?

(Above) : During the afternoon of 7 September, DRS Class 20/3 No. 20307 fails at Bridgwater on 6M67, nuclear flask working to Crewe. As the safety case for these trains requires that 2 locomotives must be operative before it commences its journey, something had to be obtained to get the flasks back up north. This being the case, Freightliner's Class 66/6 No. 66620 was unusually summoned and the ensemble (66620+20307+37605 with 3 FNAs) is seen passing Defford 45 minutes late.   *(Peter Tandy)*

Infrastructure Changes

To allow more intermodal services to serve Southampton Western Docks, ballast trains are no longer being loaded there. Eastleigh now receives ballast from Grain via a new overnight train from Hoo Junction, while Westbury has a direct service from Mountsorrel, operated by EWS:

   6Z50, 10:33 (SX) Mountsorrel - Westbury VQ   6Z51, 19:30 (SX) Westbury VQ - Mountsorrel

The services are routed via the Berks & Hants and Swindon, respectively, with the Westbury train also supplying Freightliner's newly-commissioned facility at Fairwater yard, Taunton, by a new trip working:

   6Z34, 13:18 (SX) Westbury - Fairwater Yard   6Z33, 09:55 (SX) Fairwater Yard -Westbury

(Left) : Network Rail upgrade Fairwater Yard, Taunton, making it a base for a Track Renewal train, previously based at Reading. Freightliner *Heavy Haul* also move its South West infrastructure operation to the yard, and one of the first items to move to the site is a Network Rail Track Renewal Train. Running as 6Z33, Swindon - Fairwater Yard, the train passes Worle Parkway on 25 September with No. 66622 in charge and No. 66604 out of sight 'dead-on-rear' of this very long train. The new Yard will serve as a base for forthcoming major renewal work on the West of England mainline.   *(Chris Perkins)*

OCTOBER

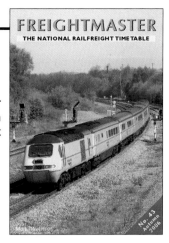

FREIGHTMASTER
THE NATIONAL RAILFREIGHT TIMETABLE

North Blyth Coal

The growth in imported coal continues to gather pace as yet another East Coast port is now dispatching imported coal by rail (the first train actually ran on Monday, 18 September) from the new coal import terminal at North Blyth.

One train a day will run initially, as follows:

6C14, 14.:23 (SX) North Blyth - Eggborough
4N04, 08:30 (SX) Drax - North Blyth

The 'new' coal terminal is on the branch that leads to Alcan's Ship Unloading Facility (SUF) at North Blyth, about half a mile south of the now derelict motive power depot at Cambois. The location is called 'Battleship Wharf', and is run / owned by the Port of Blyth. The trains join the Lynemouth & Ashington to Bedlington line at Winning Crossing triangle, then goes on to Newcastle (Blyth & Tyne) via Newsham and Palmersville to Benton Junction, where it joins the ECML near to Heaton depot.

Humber TEA's

(Right) : Humber Oil Refinery take delivery of new 100-tonne VTG (TEA) petroleum bogie tanks for use on the Humber - Kingsbury/Jarrow circuit, such as No. VTG 88144 seen at Kingsbury. *(Martin Buck)*

(Below) : A rake of Seven new TEA's form the consist of 6Z50, Wembley - Immingham on 12 October. The train is passing Huddersfield on the ECML hauled by One-liveried Class 47/8 No. 47818. *(John Rudd)*

Leaf Busters

Yes, it's that time again, autumn arrives and Network Rail start their annual war on leaf fall. As usual, all the Railfreight Operators are involved in providing traction for the RHTT train sets, but EWS lose some duties to DRS and GBRf, the latter entering the fray for the first time, albeit with a single working.

(Above) : RHTT vehicles are coded FEA-F and the problem of leaf fall is tackled by using a mix of high pressure water jets and Sandite application. Spraying is underway as DRS Class 37/0 Nos. 37059 and 37069 top & tail 3J96, the 14:49 Holyhead - Chester leg of the day's itinerary, seen passing Holywell Junction on 7 October, running about 70-minutes late. *(Alan Sherratt)*

(Below) : These trains are a real bonus to rail enthusiasts as they bring motive power to parts of the country not normally associated with the class. Here, Class 20/3 Nos. 20307 & 20306 pass through Brandon on the Ely - Norwich mainline with 1Z61, 09:10 Stowmarket - Trowse 'Water Cannon'. The date is 16 October and the train is on a stretch of track which is still controlled by semaphore signalling. *(Nigel Gibbs)*

(Above) : Here we feature the sole GBRf working - 3J31, 03:49 Hornsey - Finsbury Park RHTT - which goes via Welwyn Garden City, Hertford North and Foxton. 'Metronet' liveried Class 66/7 No. 66722 brings up the rear with No. 66719 atop as 3J31 passes through Grange Park station on 3 October. *(Nigel Gibbs)*

(Below) : Not the most remarkable of photograph of an EWS RHTT train, but included to mark when Greenpeace campaigners scale the 650ft. tower at Didcot Power Station on 2 November to protest against fossil fuel emissions. The words 'Blair's Legacy' is daubed on the tower, although barely discernible as a white paint stain on the stack above the rear cab end of Class 66/0 No. 66218 which, along with No. 66179, heads for the refuelling point with one of the Didcot-based RHTT sets. *(Martin Buck)*

Autumn Highlander

(Above) : On Friday, 6 October, 'Deltic' No. 55022 *Royal Scots Grey* sets off from London King's Cross on a four day tour to the far north of Scotland but suffers a power unit failure when a piston goes through the crankcase, resulting in the Deltic limping to Edinburgh on one engine, where WCRC's No. 47245 and the CFPS's No. 40145 take over on the two-day trip to the Kyle of Lochalsh and Thurso. On 9 October, the tour heads back to the Capital with the 'Whistler' working all the way from Inverness and the Deltic attached inside at Perth. The Deltic is shut down at Newcastle and with it 'dead in tow', the cavalcade is seen passing East Cowton, running as 1Z25, 08:10 Inverness - King's Cross. *(Andrew Naylor)*

DRS Diversity

(Top Right) : During Autumn, DRS hire a number of Riviera Class 47s pending delivery of 'Dreds' Nos. 66414 - 66420 from Canada; those still in Virgin colours are repainted into Riviera's Oxford blue, similar to DRS's blue, and some renamed. Two of the repainted locos, 47843 *Vulcan* & 47848 *Titan Star* pass Hest Bank on 26 October with the weekly 6C52 Heysham - Sellafield flask train.

(Centre Right) : Two of the latest batch of brand new Class 66/4 locomotives, Nos. 66417 and 66414 make their debut on 2 November with the weekly 6C51, Sellafield - Heysham flasks, seen leaving Arnside.

(Bottom Right) : No. 47853 *Rail Express*, still in its 'heritage' XP64 uniform, approaches Carnforth on 24 October with 6K73, Sellafield - Crewe flasks. *(All Andrew Naylor)*

Sandblower 'Spin & Win'

(Below) : Litlington, on the Hitchin to Royston main line, is the setting for EWS Class 60 No. 60034 as it heads 1Z27, 06:40 Bristol Temple Meads - Ely charter (to Middleton Towers) on 21 October. Class 57 No. 57012 *Freightliner Envoy* will be attached to the rear of the train at Ely. *(Nigel Gibbs)*

'Aluminium 100'

(Above) : Following it's reinstatement to allow the withdrawal of sister-locomotive Class 37/4 No. 37425, No. 37410 *Aluminium 100* is moved DIT to South Wales and it first two outings are shake down runs on the Bristol East Depot steel trip working. It's seen here at Newport on the second day of working (24 October) with the return 6C02, Bristol East Depot - Newport ADJ empties. *(Chris Perkins)*

FHH Machen Stone

(Below) : Changing times ahead? EWS, in conjunction with MendipRail, is the main traction provider for aggregate traffic emanating from the Mendip quarries. However, on 24 October, Freightliner Class 66/5 No. 66515 works from Whatley Quarry to Machen (6Z78) in readiness to work 6Z79, 11:45 Machen Quarry - Allington loaded Hanson Hoppers, photographed in transit through Newport station. *(Chris Perkins)*

Middleton 'Skips'

(Above) : There are some freight services which are diagrammed for Class 66/0 haulage and seldom see anything else. However, 27 October proves to be the exception for 6L98, Peterborough Yard - Middleton Towers empty sand hoppers as a pair of Class 67 locomotives are unusually allocated to work the train! Camera in hand, the photographer moves swiftly to capture the train as it passes Ely on the outward journey, seen on an embankment above flooded fields, headed by Nos. 67029 + 67016.   *(John Rudd)*

(Below) : The added bonus is that one of the train locomotives is celebrity 'Skip' No. 67029, which is seen again at Middleton Towers passing over a manually controlled level crossing with the return (6E88) working to Peterborough. The Hepworth Minerals glassworks (destination for 6L98) is accessed via a single track 'freight only' line, 3-miles out of Kings Lynn.   *(John Rudd)*

IZAs to Store

(Above) : Stock moves are popular among railway photographers and 24 October makes a welcome change from the staple diet of passenger and DVT stock moving to Long Marston. Class 47/7 No. 47714 heads a rake of IZA wagons at Fladbury, forming 6Z84, Bescot - Long Marston. *(Peter Tandy)*

GBRf 'Metronet' Work

The weekend of 11/12 November sees another period of intensive engineering work on the London Underground Metropolitan Line with GBRf providing eight trains for Metronet. The work being carried out involves the removal of limestone ballast and replacing with fresh granite ballast, plus the laying of concrete sleepers and continuous welded rail. The train details are listed to provide readers with a better idea of the number of engineering trains needed to support such major infrastructure work.

      6M60, 22:30 (Fri)   Wellingborough Yard - Mantles Wood

      6M61, 00:20 (Sat)   Wellingborough Yard - Mantles Wood

      6M62, 02:10 (Sat)   Wellingborough Yard - Harrow on the Hill

      6M63, 03:00 (Sat)   Tonbridge - Harrow on the Hill

      6M64, 05:40 (Sat)   Ferme Park - Harrow on the Hill

      6M65, 06:10 (Sat)   Wellingborough Yard - Harrow on the Hill

      6M66, 16:00 (Sat)   Ferme Park - Harrow on the Hill

      6M67, 11:00 (Sun)   Ferme Park - Harrow on the Hill

In addition, the following trains run in the lead up to the weekend to bring in materials for the above:

      6J10, 07:00 (Mon)   Wellingborough yard - Castleton
      6M20, 09:10 (Tues) Castleton - Wellingborough yard

      6M30, 13:10 (Wed)   Wellingborough yard - Washwood Heath cemex
      6M40, 05:55 (Fri)   Washwood Heath cemex - Wellingborough yard

      6O61, 14:47 (WThO) Ferme Park - Grain
      6E71, 22:20 (WThO) Grain - Ferme Park

(Above) : As previously mentioned, several trains run in connection with the LUL engineering work bringing in materials including new rails from Castleton in Greater Manchester. Class 66/7 No. 66717 draws forward onto the mainline before propelling the empty wagons (6J10) into the Corus rail sidings at Castleton on 4 December. The train originates from Wellingborough and will return there the following day (6M20) with rails for the Metronet LUL work. *(Alan Sherratt)*

(Below) : For the record, 'Metronet' Class 66/7 No. 66719 was the first of its class to work onto LUL metals and here's the proof, photographed at Amersham on 19 August, having arrived with 6M60, 23:30 Wellingborough - Harrow on the Hill. *(John Stretton)*

VFM Railfreight

(Above) : On 2 November, a new intermodal service between Hams Hall and Mossend is introduced under the "VFM Railfreight" brand, a joint venture between FM Rail and Victa Railfreight Limited. The commodities carried in ISO Containers or Swap Bodies include thermalite blocks, white and perishable goods. Additional new freight traffic soon joins the trunk service, when the movement of prestigious motorcars in ex-FGW Motorail vans is added later in the month. The luxury vehicles are transported via a new feeder service from Long Marston in Warwickshire for auction in Scotland with a corresponding southbound service returning 'off-lease' motorcars. On Monday, 20 November, FM Rail Class 47/0 No. 47145 *Myrddin Emrys* arrives at Evesham with 8 NVAs Nos. 96605, 96608, 96606, 96602, 96607, 96604, 96609 & 96603, en route to Long Marston. *(Don Gatehouse)*

'Platinum' Princess

(Top) : Seventy years to the day since its record-breaking non-stop runs from London Euston to Glasgow and back, Princess Royal Class 4-6-2 steam locomotive No. 6201 *Princess Elizabeth* works a two day Kingfisher charter over the northern WCML to commemorate its 1936 exploits. On 16 November, she takes the 'Mid-Day Scot', originating at Birmingham International, from Preston (dep. 10:09hrs) to Glasgow (due 18:32hrs). The train is due to make a pathing stop at Carnforth from 10:42hrs until 11:13hrs, but as No. 6201 is in fine fettle she charges through Carnforth non-stop, passing Class 66/4s Nos. 66412 and 66413 in the loop working 3J06 Water Cannon train. *(Andrew Naylor)*

(Above) : After stopping for water at Oxenholme, No. 6201 still runs early and she is seen climbing past Salterwath towards Shap Summit, almost 40 minutes ahead of time. *(Andrew Naylor)*

Acid Finale

(Left) : Class 66/4 No. 66414 passes Barton and Broughton loop with the final working of acid tanks from Albion Chemicals at Sandbach to Sellafield on 3 November. Future deliveries of acid will be coming from Billingham on Teeside via the daily EWS 'Enterprise' service to Carlisle for onward movement by DRS to Sellafield. The locomotive travelled light engine to Sandbach to pick up the tanks, which is believed to be the first (and last) time a DRS 66 had worked this train. *(Alan Sherratt)*

Hitchin Scrap

(Above) : As the crow flies .... certainly doesn't apply to 6Z74, Cardiff Tidal - Hitchin loaded scrap (ex-6Z93) which follows a bizarre route via Gloucester, Water Orton, Nuneaton, Melton Mowbray, Peterborough, Ely and Royston in order to reach its destination. On 21 November, Class 66/0 No. 66189 passes through Whittlesea with 6Z74, a most unusual, but welcome, freight flow for the March line!   *(John Rudd)*

'Jumbo' Coal

(Below) : The shape of things to come .... in February this year, EWS ran a 'US-style' coal train, totalling over 4,000 tonnes, from Carlisle to Gascoigne Wood, effectively coupling two normal HTA train sets together, hauled by a pair of Class 66/0 locomotives. The trial was deemed a success, the only problem being a lack of pathing loops long enough to accommodate such trains! On 22 November, a further trial takes place using Nos. 66218 + 66094 and the pair are seen passing South Otterington, near Northallerton, with 6L65, Carlisle Yard - York.   *(Ian Ball)*